A MILITARY MOTHER'S 90-DAY GUIDE TO A GREATER CONNECTION WITH HER DAUGHTER

Written By: Charise Freeman
Illustrations By: Le'Mia Spencer

1

Ordering Information:
Quantity sales. Special discounts are available on quantity purchases by corporations, associations, and others. For details, contact the "Special Sales Department" at the email address above.

Growing In Love Together – A Military Mother's 90-day Guide to a Greater Connection with Her Daughter / Charise Freeman —1st ed.

ISBN 979-8-9852975-0-8

CONTENTS

INTRO 5
GUIDE FOR THE GUIDE 9
DAY 1 11
DAY 11 22
DAY 21 32
DAY 31 44
DAY 41 55
DAY 51 66
DAY 61 77
DAY 71 88
DAY 81 99
REFLECTION 110
ACKNOWLEDGEMENTS 112

*This book is dedicated to God, my Big Onion, my Lil'
Onion, my Pineapple, and my Melon.*

Where it All Began

In 2011, during my last deployment to Oman AB, it hit me hard when I realized I knew nothing about my 5-year-old daughter. I would have to call the caregiver(s) to get even the most basic information such as what her favorite food was. I loved the Air Force but when I realized I had a hard time reconnecting with my daughter after deployments, I knew something had to change. Deep down I knew I wanted something different, something better than me and my mom had. So, I decided to leave the active duty Air Force and focus on our relationship. At the time, I felt it was the only way to really focus on our relationship because the lack of tools for reintegration caused us to become more and more distant each time I returned home.

Within days of my separation date, I did all the things! Took her to the zoo, got her nails done, took her out to eat, smiled and took pictures for Facebook. I felt like we were connecting more because I had more time with her, and she seemed super happy about all the things I did for her. Everything was right in my world until...it wasn't.

After nearly 1.5 years of being unemployed, searching and applying for jobs, I finally got an interview! On May 24, 2013, I went to an interview for the job of my dreams. Based on how the interview had gone, I just KNEW I had that job IN THE BAG. After the interview, I looked at my phone and saw I had a voicemail from my daughter's school asking me to call the school immediately. I called, they put the principal on the phone. My heart sank as I listened to the principal informing me that my daughter made a statement about wanting to harm herself and that she was put on a hold in a facility since they couldn't get ahold of me. My world came crashing down. I was angry at my daughter. I was angry at the school. I was confused.

Each day that passed that she was in that facility, I cried out to God and reached out to my church family for help in that very troubling time in my life. My church family held me close, and God held me closer as I began my long journey of reevaluation, connection, forgiveness, and willingness. I signed up for parenting classes, counseling for me, counseling for her, and counseling for us. I discovered that she felt like I loved her brother more than her. After coming out of the state of confusion (I truly did not understand how she felt that way) I realized it was not my job to necessarily understand HOW she could feel that way. It was my job to validate her feelings and move accordingly. I had so much love for her, but I couldn't quite figure out how to truly SHOW her the love I felt. On my journey of changing how I showed her love I discovered that there were 5 different ways that one receives love, and some ways are more favored by the individual than the others. The 5 different ways that one receives love are through the 5 Love Languages.

I began to learn about the 5 Love Languages and took a quiz and learned that the way she received love was very different than the way I thought she received love. At the time, my daughter's top love language was physical touch. Finding that out really shed some light on why she felt like I didn't love her—I was not the hugging, holding, cuddling type. Doing so made me uncomfortable because of my past and being sexually abused as a child. I had no idea what HEALTHY family love looked like other than giving material things. Knowing this, I put my pride and the need to want to do things the way I thought they should be done aside and began to connect in a different way that didn't just involve material things.

Knowing her top love language and wanting to strengthen our connection I made it my mission, no matter how uncomfortable, to love her in the way that she best received love. When I say I had to get uncomfortable, I mean it. I would cringe inside and out at even the thought of hugging her for more than the 4 seconds that she hugged me before bed. I had to teach myself that physical touch was not a bad thing when done healthily, and it is what my daughter needed. I started out by hugging her a little longer before bed which evolved into letting her lay on my shoulder while watching tv, and then eventually led to holding her as she laid on my shoulder.

I know that it isn't easy to adjust to what your kids need especially when it makes you uncomfortable. That is why I wrote this daily connection guide! This guide outlines inexpensive things you can do daily to connect with your daughter using the 5 Love Languages. This guide takes the guess work out of what to do each day and majority of the tasks are done in 30 minutes or less. The main idea is to do something DAILY. Consistency builds trust and trust is definitely something you need for a solid foundation of your relationship with her.

My journey to intentionally connect with my daughter started 8 years ago and back then I made a commitment to myself that looked something like this:

I will connect daily.

I will be better than I was yesterday.

I will push past the uncomfortable.

I will show her love, unconditionally.

That commitment still stands today. Connection is a choice that I make daily because I'm in it for the long haul and I want nothing but the best for our relationship. We are Growing In Love Together (G.I.L.T.).

Before you get started, make a commitment to yourself, and take note of it below:

I will:

____

____

____

____

____

____

Guide for the Guide

DAY:
The day you are on

Task for the day

Time:
The approx. amount of time the task for the day will take

Love Language(s) in Action:
This refers to the 5 Love Languages. The 5 Love Languages give insight about the way each person receives love. No matter what your daughter's top love language is, showing all 5 Love Languages is important which is why I have included ways to speak to each language.

Connection Tip: *This is a tip on how to do the task for the day or a way to add to the task for the day to speak to more Love Languages.*

Guide for the Guide Continued...

Each Love Language and how it is spoken:

Acts of Service: *doing something for her that she would normally have to do herself*

Quality Time: *giving your undivided attention while spending time with her*

Receiving Gifts: *Giving her a thoughtful gift*

Words of Affirmation: *Express how amazing she is and WHY*

Physical Touch: *Hugs, high fives, cuddles, etc.*

DAY 1

Make her bed for her

Time: *5 mins*

Love Language(s) in Action: *Acts of Service*

Connection Tip: *Let her know you are going to make her bed up for her. If she inquires, just let her know you want to show her love.*

DAY 2

Help her pick up her toys

Time: 15 mins

Love Language(s) in Action: *Acts of Service, Quality Time*

Connection Tip: *Make it into a game by setting a timer!*

DAY 3:

Make her favorite meal

Time: *30 mins*

Love Language(s) in Action: *Acts of Service*

Connection Tip: *Let her know you'd like to make her favorite meal and ask her what she would like you to make*

DAY 4:

Give her a high five

Time: 5 minutes

Love Language(s) in Action: Physical Touch

Connection Tip: Don't tie it to anything she has done, just simply give her a high five.

DAY 5:

Lock arms with her

Time: 15 minutes

Love Language(s) in Action: Physical Touch

Connection Tip: If/when she begins to speak, listen intently.

DAY 6:

Lay your head on her lap while watching a show that interests her

Time: 30 minutes

Love Language(s) in Action: Physical Touch, Quality Time

Connection Tip: Once the show is over, talk about the show and take turns sharing your thoughts.

DAY 7:

Praise her in front of others

Time: *5 minutes*

Love Language(s) in Action: *Words of Affirmation*

Connection Tip: *Others could be siblings, parent, friends, etc. The point is to praise her out loud for others to hear.*

DAY 8:

Compliment her before you correct her

Time: 5 minutes

Love Language(s) in Action: *Words of Affirmation*

Connection Tip: *Don't let her "doing it wrong" overshadow the fact that she tried.*

DAY 9:

Write a letter saying why you are so proud of her

Time: 30 minutes

Love Language(s) in Action: *Words of Affirmation*

Connection Tip: *The letter doesn't have to be long but, write from the heart.*

DAY 10:

Brush your teeth with her

Time: *5 minutes*

Love Language(s) in Action: Quality Time

Connection Tip: *Sometimes there are no words that need to be said. Just be.*

"You're further than you were before. Keep going."

– Charise Freeman

DAY 11:

Be attentive to what she is doing and be engaged

Time: 15 minutes

Love Language(s) in Action: Quality Time

Connection Tip: Put your phone down.

DAY 12:

Play a board game

Time: 30 minutes

Love Language(s) in Action: Quality Time

Connection Tip: Let her pick the game you play.

DAY 13:

Clean her room for her

Time: 15 minutes

Love Language(s) in Action: Acts of Service

Connection Tip: If she wants to play after you cleaned it, let her.

DAY 14:

Wrap her favorite snack and watch her open it

Time: *15 minutes*

Love Language(s) in Action: *Receiving Gifts*

Connection Tip: *The gift can be a snack you've had in your room. You keep telling yourself you will eat it one day. Wrap it and give it to her.*

DAY 15:

Write a letter and mail it

Time: *30 minutes*

Love Language(s) in Action: Receiving Gifts, Words of Affirmation

Connection Tip: *Write it on a piece of paper in her favorite color.*

DAY 16:

Pick her up on time

Time: 5 minutes

Love Language(s) in Action: Acts of Service

Connection Tip: Hold yourself accountable by telling her what time you will be picking her up.

DAY 17:

Hide a gift for her to find

Time: 15 minutes

Love Language(s) in Action: *Receiving Gifts*

Connection Tip: *Give her clues to help with the search.*

DAY 18:

Invite her to do a random act of kindness

Time: *30 minutes*

Love Language(s) in Action: *Acts of Service*

Connection Tip: *After the experience, talk to her about it and get her thoughts.*

DAY 19:

Listen to her favorite song

Time: *5 minutes*

Love Language(s) in Action: *Physical Touch, Quality Time*

Connection Tip: *Put it on repeat, look up the lyrics, and sing along.*

DAY 20:

Hold her hand as she speaks

Time: 15 minutes

Love Language(s) in Action: Physical Touch, Quality Time

Connection Tip: It may get uncomfortable, breathe through it.

"Remove the 'U' in guilt and G.I.L.T., Grow In Love Together"

– Charise Freeman

DAY 21:

Do an art project together

Time: 30 minutes

Love Language(s) in Action: Quality Time

Connection Tip: Gift them to each other.

DAY 22:

Shower her with 5 compliments

Time: 5 minutes

Love Language(s) in Action: Words of Affirmation

Connection Tip: Compliment her in front of others.

DAY 23:

Write a note saying you are proud of her

Time: 15 minutes

Love Language(s) in Action: Words of Affirmation

Connection Tip: Write it on paper that is her favorite color.

DAY 24:

Write a letter expressing what you love about her

Time: *30 minutes*

Love Language(s) in Action: *Words of Affirmation*

Connection Tip: *Place it in an envelope.*

DAY 25:

Write notes and leave them on her mirror

Time: 5 minutes

Love Language(s) in Action: Words of Affirmation

Connection Tip: *The note can be about anything!*

DAY 26:

Give her your undivided attention

Time: 15 minutes

Love Language(s) in Action: Quality Time

Connection Tip: No multitasking.

DAY 27:

Eat dinner together

Time: 30 minutes

Love Language(s) in Action: Quality Time

Connection Tip: Make the meal together.

DAY 28:

Say encouraging words to her

Time: 5 minutes

Love Language(s) in Action: Words of Affirmation

Connection Tip: Aim to encourage her even when she isn't having a hard time.

DAY 29:

Have breakfast with her

Time: 15 minutes

Love Language(s) in Action: Quality Time

Connection Tip: *No need to say anything. There is nothing wrong with sitting in silence.*

DAY 30:

Run errands with her

Time: 30 minutes

Love Language(s) in Action: Quality Time

Connection Tip: Resist the temptation to just get things done in a hurry and bring her along. Trust me, it won't add that much time to your errand run.

"It's not about how a child relates to you... Its about how you relate to the child"

– Unknown

DAY 31:

Tuck her in bed

Time: 5 minutes

Love Language(s) in Action: Quality Time, Acts of Service, Physical Touch

Connection Tip: Comment on something awesome she did today.

DAY 32:

Clean her room with her

Time: 15 minutes

Love Language(s) in Action: Quality Time

Connection Tip: Make it a game by setting a timer.

DAY 33:

Prepare her favorite snack and bring it to her

Time: 30 minutes

Love Language(s) in Action: Acts of Service

Connection Tip: Eat a snack in her room with her.

DAY 34:

Give her a piggyback ride

Time: 5 minutes

Love Language(s) in Action: Physical Touch, Quality Time

Connection Tip: Have fun with it.

DAY 35:

Create 1 move of a secret handshake

Time: 15 minutes

Love Language(s) in Action: Quality Time, Physical Touch

Connection Tip: Don't over complicate it.

DAY 36:

Hold hands while on a walk

Time: 30 minutes

Love Language(s) in Action: Physical Touch, Quality Time

Connection Tip: Ask her about her day.

DAY 37:

Brush her hair

Time: 5 minutes

Love Language(s) in Action: Physical Touch, Quality Time, Acts of Service

Connection Tip: Ask her about the dream she had last night

DAY 38:

Take a car ride

Time: 15 minutes

Love Language(s) in Action: Quality Time

Connection Tip: Sit in silence (No music. No phone calls) and let her start a conversation.

DAY 39:

Cook a meal together

Time: 30 minutes

Love Language(s) in Action: Quality Time

Connection Tip: *Ask her what she wants to be when she grows up.*

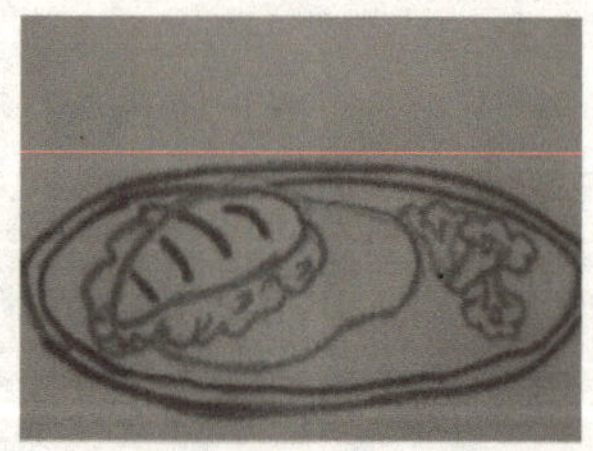

DAY 40:

Hold her hand and sit in silence

Time: 5 minutes

Love Language(s) in Action: Quality Time, Physical Touch

Connection Tip: Silence is golden. It may get uncomfortable and that is okay. You've got this.

"Respond to your PURPOSE, not your feelings"

– Caneisha Thrower

DAY 41:

Jump rope together

Time: *15 minutes*

Love Language(s) in Action: *Quality Time*

Connection Tip: *Take turns counting each other's jumps.*

DAY 42:

Play a game with her after her scheduled bedtime

Time: 30 minutes

Love Language(s) in Action: Quality Time

Connection Tip: Don't get hung up on routine, color outside of the lines a little, mom.

DAY 43:

Say how proud you are of her

Time: 5 minutes

Love Language(s) in Action: *Words of Affirmation*

Connection Tip: *Tell her why.*

DAY 44:

Just be there for her and be present.

Time: 15 minutes

Love Language(s) in Action: Quality Time

Connection Tip: *Sit in her room while she is getting ready for the day.*

DAY 45:

Cuddle/snuggle with her

Time: 30 minutes

Love Language(s) in Action: Quality Time, Acts of Service

Connection Tip: Read a book to her.

DAY 46:

Ask her to teach you a trending move

Time: *5 minutes*

Love Language(s) in Action: Quality Time

Connection Tip: *Have fun with it. Be goofy.*

DAY 47:

Call and ask her what the most exciting part of her day was

Time: 15 minutes

Love Language(s) in Action: Quality Time

Connection Tip: Stay engaged. Comment on what she tells you.

DAY 48:

Practice a sport with her

Time: 30 minutes

***Love Language(s) in Action:* Quality Time**

***Connection Tip:* Be okay with looking foolish and laugh together.**

DAY 49:

Write a love note

Time: 5 minutes

Love Language(s) in Action: *Words of Affirmation*

Connection Tip: Don't overthink it, just write.

DAY 50:

Offer a shoulder massage

Time: 15 minutes

Love Language(s) in Action: Quality Time, Physical Touch

Connection Tip: Don't be offended if she declines. Remember, its not about YOU.

"Come alongside her and let her know that your love for her does not stop because she has not made the bed up to your standards."

– Charise Freeman, Growing in love together podcast ep. 25

DAY 51:

Hold her hand while you drive

Time: 30 minutes

Love Language(s) in Action: *Physical Touch, Quality Time*

Connection Tip: *It's gonna be wierd. Just go with it.*

DAY 52:

Practice your secret handshake and add another move

Time: 5 minutes

Love Language(s) in Action: Quality Time, Physical Touch

Connection Tip: Ask her if she'd like to choose the next move or if she'd like you to choose.

DAY 53:

Have a dance party

Time: 15 minutes

Love Language(s) in Action: Quality Time

Connection Tip: *Create a playlist with each other's favorite songs and hit shuffle.*

DAY 54:

Build a fort together

Time: 30 minutes

Love Language(s) in Action: Quality Time

Connection Tip: Let her take the lead.

DAY 55:

Pick a flower from outside and give it to her

Time: 5 minutes

Love Language(s) in Action: Receiving Gifts

Connection Tip: Write a note with it "a gift for the most beautiful girl in the world'

DAY 56:

Mail her a postcard

Time: 15 minutes

Love Language(s) in Action: Receiving Gifts

Connection Tip: Find one with her favorite
character on it

DAY 57:

Send her on a gift treasure hunt

Time: *30 minutes*

Love Language(s) in Action: *Quality Time, Receiving Gifts*

Connection Tip: *Write clues on pieces of paper and put them where she will randomly find them.*

DAY 58:

Write notes to each other and pass them back and forth throughout the day

Time: 5 minutes

Love Language(s) in Action: Quality Time

Connection Tip: Find a neutral place to put the notes

DAY 59:

Write a letter expressing what you love about her

Time: 15 minutes

Love Language(s) in Action: Words of Affirmation

Connection Tip: Write it on a paper that is her favorite color

DAY 60:

Make her favorite food

Time: 30 minutes

Love Language(s) in Action: Acts of Service

Connection Tip: Ask her what food she would like you to make.

"My daughter and I may have an amazing relationship but let me be the first to tell you it takes WORK. Some days are harder than others but overall its soooooo rewarding. She is blossoming into a wonderful young lady. I love her so so much!"

– Charise Freeman

DAY 61:

Put toothpaste on her toothbrush

Time: 5 minutes

Love Language(s) in Action: *Acts of Service*

Connection Tip: *Brush your teeth with her.*

DAY 62:

Paint her nails

Time: 15 minutes

Love Language(s) in Action: Quality Time, Acts of Service

Connection Tip: Give her a little massage to go along with her manicure/pedicure.

DAY 63:

Work on a project with her

Time: 30 minutes

Love Language(s) in Action: Quality Time, Acts of Service

Connection Tip: Let it get messy. Set a timer.

DAY 64:

Give a family group hug

Time: *Less than 5 minutes*

Love Language(s) in Action: **Physical Touch**

Connection Tip: *Ask her if she wants to join a group hug. Don't be disappointed or force her to if she doesn't want to.*

DAY 65:

Hold her hand while you ask a question

Time: 15 minutes

***Love Language(s) in Action:* Physical Touch, Quality Time**

***Connection Tip:* Look her in the eye as you speak and when she speaks**

DAY 66:

Read her favorite book

Time: 30 minutes

Love Language(s) in Action: Physical Touch, Acts of Service, Quality Time

Connection Tip: Cuddle with her.

DAY 67:

Practice your secret handshake and create another move

Time: 5 minutes

Love Language(s) in Action: Quality Time, Physical Touch

Connection Tip: Ask her what move is her favorite.

DAY 68:

Play a card game together

Time: 15 minutes

Love Language(s) in Action: Quality Time

Connection Tip: Play 1 game you used to play as a kid or play 1 game of her choice.

DAY 69:

Tell her how your day was

Time: 15 minutes

Love Language(s) in Action: Quality Time

Connection Tip: Be honest as possible about your day. Show you are human.

DAY 70:

Give her a huge bear hug for at least 20 seconds

Time: Less than 5 minutes

Love Language(s) in Action: Physical Touch

Connection Tip: Ask her if she can give you a hug and don't be upset about the answer if it is no. Just chill.

"Striving to be better than my mom was my downfall... once I focused on being better than I was yesterday, I released bitterness and things became clearer."

– Charise Freeman

DAY 71:

Bake cookies together

Time: 15 minutes

Love Language(s) in Action: Quality Time

Connection Tip: Let her lead the conversation.

DAY 72:

Come up with a cheer or song with her name in it

Time: 30 minutes

Love Language(s) in Action: Words of Affirmation

Connection Tip: This could be a song that exists and you insert her name or a song that has been completely made up by you.

DAY 73:

Express gratitude for a gift she has given to you

Time: 5 minutes

Love Language(s) in Action: Words of Affirmation

Connection Tip: Express why you are grateful for the gift.

DAY 74:

Draw a picture for her and put it in an envelope

Time: 15 minutes

Love Language(s) in Action: Receiving Gifts

Connection Tip: *Tell her why you chose to draw the picture and what it means to you.*

DAY 75:

Do a puzzle together

Time: 30 minutes

Love Language(s) in Action: *Quality Time*

Connection Tip: *Come up with a strategy together for completing the puzzle.*

DAY 76:

Tie her shoes for her

Time: *Less than 5 minutes*

Love Language(s) in Action: *Acts of Service*

Connection Tip: *Tell her about how you learned to tie your shoe or tell her about how you taught her how to tie hers.*

DAY 77:

Help her do a house contribution (aka chore)

Time: 15 minutes

Love Language(s) in Action: Acts of Service, Quality Time

Connection Tip: Ask her which house contribution she would like your help with.

DAY 78:

Go for a hike/walk together

Time: 30 minutes

Love Language(s) in Action: Quality Time

Connection Tip: Stop to have a picnic at your destination or along the way.

DAY 79:

Touch her shoulder as you pass her by

Time: *Less than 5 minutes*

Love Language(s) in Action: *Physical Touch*

Connection Tip: *No words needed.*

DAY 80:

Tickle her

Time: 15 minutes

Love Language(s) in Action: Physical Touch, Quality Time

Connection Tip: If she despises tickling, find a way to laugh together.

"No matter how bad the day/experience/obstacle is you can get through it. There is hope on the other side. You are a strong woman. You've got this."

–Charise Freeman

DAY 81:

Let her do your hair/makeup

Time: 30 minutes

Love Language(s) in Action: Quality Time, Physical Touch

Connection Tip: Let that be your look for the day.

DAY 82:

Practice all the moves you have of your secret handshake

Time: 5 minutes

Love Language(s) in Action: Quality Time, Physical Touch

Connection Tip: Celebrate your success

DAY 83:

Paint each other's nails

Time: 30 minutes

Love Language(s) in Action: Quality Time, Physical Touch

Connection Tip: Let her choose your nail color for you.

DAY 84:

Do house contributions together

Time: 30 minutes

Love Language(s) in Action: Quality Time, Acts of Service

Connection Tip: Give her a choice of which house contributions she'd like to do together

DAY 85:

Buy her favorite candy and wrap it

Time: 5 minutes

Love Language(s) in Action: Receiving Gifts

Connection Tip: Ask her to name her top 3 favorite candies so there is an element of surprise when she opens the gift.

DAY 86:

Ask her opinion about an outfit you are choosing

Time: 15 minutes

Love Language(s) in Action: Quality Time

Connection Tip: *Wear what she recommends*

DAY 87:

Make homemade pizza together

Time: 30 minutes

Love Language(s) in Action: Quality Time

Connection Tip: Email
Charise@growinginlovetogether.com *for an easy
and frugal recipe online.*

DAY 88:

Say affirmations together

Time: *5 minutes*

Love Language(s) in Action: *Quality Time*

Connection Tip: *Speak affirmations over one another*

DAY 89:

Send her a gift through the mail

Time: 15 minutes

Love Language(s) in Action: Receiving Gifts

Connection Tip: Write a note telling her why you gifted her the item(s).

DAY 90:

Have a sleepover in her room

Time: *1 – 2 hours*

Love Language(s) in Action: *Quality Time*

Connection Tip: *Start the sleepover an hour or more before bedtime to allow some time for talking with one another.*

"On this journey of Growing In Love Together, remind yourself that perfection is a myth. On this path to growth you will make mistakes. The most important thing is to be kind to yourself. You are right where you need to be"

– Charise Freeman, Moms of Daughters Connection Guide, pg. 3

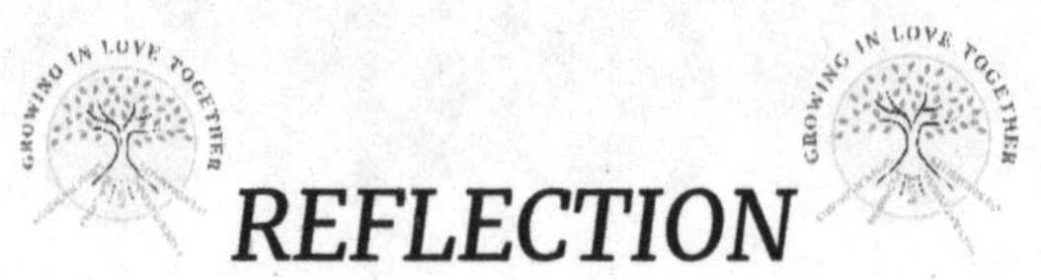

REFLECTION

It's time to reflect on what you have observed during your 90-day connection journey, what worked, what didn't work, how you plan to continue, etc.

____

____

____

____

____

____

____

____

____

____

REFLECTION

Continued...

ACKNOWLEDGEMENTS

Writing a book truly takes a village. Tremendous thanks to...

God, for never leaving my side through this whole book writing journey and this journey called life.

Dee (my lovely man), for ALWAYS being there, loving me, supporting me, and setting his dreams aside as I pursue mine.

Le'Mia, for her lovely illustrations, inspiration, and love. Keep doing what you love no matter how often it changes.

Dwayne, for saying "You're going to be famous!" when I told you I was writing a book. Those words pushed me to keep going so I could show you that ANYTHING is possible. Don't give up. I can't wait to help you publish yours.

Aunty Darese, for reminding me, in the most loving way, to keep God first in all that I do.

Shauna, for being one of my biggest cheerleaders, always.

Caneisha, for being the very first person to call to congratulate me before my book writing journey officially began. Also for granting me permission to use her profound quote.

My editing crew: Dee, Taleina, and xxJACKxJILLZxx

Everyone that donated to make this book possible

And...

Approximately one million other people that I am forgetting right now. Thank you. Everyone.